Poetry Of A Lonely Queen

Ruth Inez

BookLeaf
Publishing

India | USA | UK

Poetry Of A Lonely Queen © 2024 Ruth Inez

All rights reserved.

Ruth Inez asserts the moral right to be identified as the author of this work.

Presentation by *BookLeaf Publishing*

Web: www.bookleafpub.com

E-mail: info@bookleafpub.com

ISBN: 9789363309913

First edition 2024

Thank you for the push I needed

~Mooney~

ACKNOWLEDGEMENT

To every soul I had a contract with—those who brought betrayal, heartbreak, envy, and/or lust—you made me great; you helped me Grow. And with these poems; I Now Let You Go....

Venom

Been getting dogged out by these niggas
And yeah that's cuz I let 'em
Never picked the hero
Always chase the venom.

Him

Now that I'm older I realize
My desire to love unconditionally
Had a lot of you negus
Really thinking you were "him"
Little did y'all know
You all were
Yeah
You all were not
You all were an illusion of what I thought
I mean what I knew, I wanted
You all were a mix of potential
Potential pieces of the perfect soulmate
That without your help
I could have never manifested
See, you all were kings
Just not my kings

And that's okay
You all were motivation
To become a true queen
To look at my own flaws
And stare at my own insecurities
With that being said
I guess you could say "I was him"
Just don't forget the WAS and the fact I
eventually walked away….

They miss you too

Damn I miss them
Yeah, they miss you too
Only difference is they don't really miss you
Only what you used to do
They miss you footing the bill
And stepping on shit
Like one wrong move and they knew you would
kill a bih
They miss you telling ppl how it is
Cuz they were too scared
They miss how you used to uplift them
They miss watching you turn shit around
Right when they all thought you would drown
Girl they really just miss making you look like a
clown

They miss how easy it was to take and never
give
They miss the way you made them want to live
They miss the free drugs, good food, and endless
drinks
They miss how your body feels soft like mink
So baby girl stop crying cuz they miss you more
than you think
And that's why you have to miss them
Cuz they were only there to help you eat…..

Old Me Back

They say they want the old me back
But see, that's only cuz they didn't know me yet
They didn't know I was really sad and depressed
Waking up everyday wanting to kill myself
They didn't see the pain in my heart
Or the silent cries within my eyes
They only saw the lies
The lie that I was happy
The lie that I was strong
The lie that I really had it going on
When in all actuality
All that glory goes to God
He clearly saw the real me
And still decided to hold me down
Long as I stuck to his plan

He never lied, he never left
Never made me feel less than
So in return, I didn't fold.
No matter how cold life made me feel.
I just kept pushing, praying, and trusting.
Then finally decided to heal
So naw, I can't bring the old me back
She had a very big ego
And I'm glad that's dead
She wanted to die
And I finally want to live
So I refuse to bring the old me back
Fuck that
This woman I am now
Gotta be here for her kids
So sorry, I'm not sorry
And P.S. Fuck how y'all feel.

Lucky For You

They thought I was pressed to be their friend
But in reality, I was just passionate about seeing
people win
I just didn't realize at the time that was my
soul's purpose, no matter how it ends

Girl stop lying to these ppl, your ass was lonely.
Desperate for the love you should have felt from
your mother.
Desperate for the affection your father was never
able to give
And that's okay sis, you were a child;
hat's what you were supposed to receive. Lucky
for you, TMH ALWAYS SENDS YOU WHAT
YOU NEED.

LUCKY FOR ME?
Sis you just don't know
This is what I was born to be.
An example
A sacrifice
A literal walking testimony
Yes indeed I got everything I need
It is my inheritance

The key to success hidden deep
Within me INTERNALLY
If you knew my true past
You would know and ultimately agree
I deserved that shit sis,
RESPECTFULLY!
But I get it, it took me 32 whole years to See
every rejection was literally just divine direction
So I understand the views you may perceive…..

Shit Ain't Sweet

Y'all be thinking shit sweet like skittles
Whole time I get my clothes from rainbow
Stay thinking I got it like that
Whole time God just got my back.

Set Apart

Finally understanding what it means to be set
apart
See, I was never supposed to fit in
I was designed to be the bitch who stands
outside the box
The one to help free y'all from those mental
blocks
The one to show y'all it's okay to be your
authentic self
And how to cut free from all those chains and
locks
Proof that life will be just fine even if you do
what you want
Even if it don't look like what you were taught
The epitome of *fuck-what-they-said* and *fuck
what-you-thought*
To dig deep inside

Take a look around
And say fuck that I'll go this way instead
Fear running deep
Head to the sky
And when you do that shit, do it with less pride
Zero judgment
And big bright open eyes
Not just with the 2 but all 3
Especially the one in your mind
Love them with your whole heart
Even the ones who wanted to see you die
I promise it'll make them cry
Stand up tall, defeat all the odds
Then dance on that box like you'd dance for the
Gods
Crush all those stigmas, statistics and goals
So the next generation can live trauma-free.
Weird ass flaws and all.

Depression Is Real

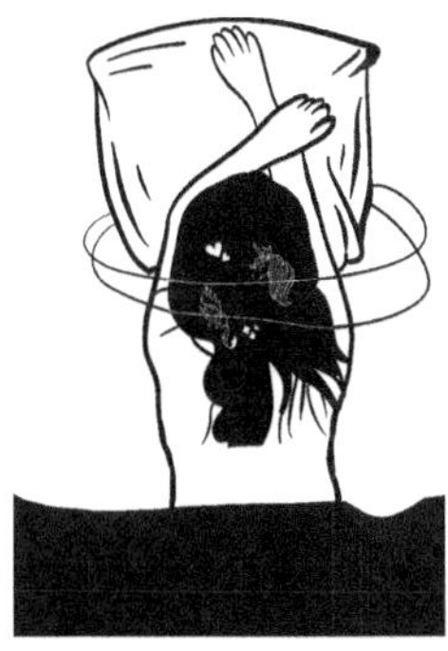

Depression is real
But a lot more manageable when you take the
time to heal.
There will still be fears,
sleepless nights,
and a lot of fucking tears
But when you do the shadow work
and change up that negative self-talk
You start to see and feel different results.
Now don't get me wrong
The rain doesn't completely stop
But eventually, you'll no longer feel like you're
drowning.
You'll finally begin to start swimming smarter
Seeing things clear
Seeing things for what they are
You begin to show up

Show out
And show em' all
This is your year to ball………

Worth Millions

Born with melanin in my skin
So I'm already worth millions
Just ain't figure out how to spend the shit yet
So I continue to plan
Continue to jot
Continue writing all these misunderstood
thoughts…

Used to cry

I used to cry because of all the pain
Now I cry because I'm overfilled by the joy and
peace I've regained
I used to cry due to all the neglect and regrets
Now I smile because I know it was all only for
my best
I used to be so angry it hurt
Now I find my jaws sore from all the laughter &
joyful outbursts
As I rise out of the dirt
I used to wake up every day ready to end it all
Now I rise up feeling grateful every morning
Knowing God wants me to ball
I used to be sad and depressed
But one day I decided to wake up every morning
and simply do my best…..

Why Do Doves Cry?

Ever wondered why doves cry?
Shit, don't trip
See, I never even took the time
To think of why
But if I had to assume
I'm pretty sure it's cuz they're tired of flying by
Yeah flying by, watching kids die
Flying by, watching humans do nothing but fuck
and lie
Tired of witnessing dreams drown in the streams
they sit by
Tired of hearing the sick feinds cry
I know if I was a dove
I'd fly fly fly
Until I reached a beautiful utopia

Or a glorious paradise far away
Where kids play with no worries
And those who are wickedly dishonest die
Where dreams prevail
And drugs aren't a thing
Unless you're out having a good time
Cuz see, where I'm from
You have no time to question such frivolous
things
Like why the eagles soar
Or did the mockingbird ever sing
And no matter how many times Prince asked our
ass
Why   do   doves   cry?
Especially when you're too busy crying your
own rivers
While wiping your own eyes
Climbing your own trees but never reaching
your dreams
And life just continues to give you more and
more big ass mountains to succeed.
So why do doves cry?
Chile, I couldn't tell you why
Cuz see, before I wrote this poem
I never really gave a fuck or 2 why
Or even had the precious time to sit and really
ponder
Hold up, wait?
Shit, y'all do doves even really cry?

Been Addicted

Been Addicted to pain
Addicted to rain
Addicted to weed
Lowkey addicted to greed
Been Addicted to boot
Addicted to looking and feeling cute
Addicted to sex
Addicted to having less
Addicted to perc, zanx's, and x
Been Addicted to friends
Addicted to foes
Addicted to fears
Addicted to tears

Addicted to the neglect I've felt all of these
years when i was feeling low
Now I'm Addicted to growth
Been Addicted to both—

Beating a nigga ass
and getting choked
Addicted to anger
Addicted to rage
Addicted to all the love I lost as I aged
Been Addicted to the grief
Addicted to the relief
Addicted to the lack of help nobody ever sees
Been Addicted to the pimps
Addicted to the players
Addicted to killers
Addicted to the drug dealers
Now I'm addicted to authentically being me and
just healing…..

Hidden Agendas

I don't trust words or actions
Cuz people gave me both at the same time
But with hidden agendas
And I can't lie that shit hurt a lil different—
Pretending to love me just to cut me
Pretending to care just to end up not being there
Pretending to be loyal
All because they could see I was royal
All because they secretly hated the parts of me
that made them awaken
And step into their divine portal
I hate the words "Sorry" and "I got you"
Cuz people said both quick
Only to do the same ol' shit
Again and again
And again

All while leaving me blowing in the wind at the
end
Just keep writing
Trying to make it all make sense…..

I'll Pass

You asked to eat my pussy
Said that's all you want
But we both know after that
Now you really gonna wanna fuck
Really gonna want to buss that nut
That's why, no matter if I was taught
To never turn down head
I'll politely have to pass
And go on instead

Fight or Flight

See, my flight or fight is a bit more meticulous
Make me feel scared? I do too much
Now I'm trying to knuck fore' you buck
Spin fore' you grin
Wipe your nose before you put a tag on MY toes
Make me feel unsure? I do too much
Just tell me what it is
Naw fr tell me what you want
And please be blunt
Money get low? I do too much
Get to praising God in advance

Be on some "Make me clap my hands"
Cuz I know he only 'bout to enhance
MY LIFE
Yeah when my life gets hard? I do too much
And go harder cuz the devil can't win
Naw, he can't make me fall
God already approved me to ball
Make me feel unheard? I do too much
Cuz when I was young I was always told to shut
up while being pushed in the cut
Make me feel protected? I do too much
Get to falling in love, and all that mushy stuff.
Then run away cuz I'm scared I'll eventually get
cut
Make me feel loved? I do too much
Get to showing that shit back
All while really being scared that shit just gonna
turn my heart all the way black
Betray me? Ima do way too much
Run to straight my alter, light a candle
And tell my ancestors how you play too much
And let them fuck you up.
Show me loyalty? I do too much
Get to feeling like I can finally trust
Like I don't have to be so tough
Show me appreciation. I do too much
Return the favor no matter the situation.
Sometimes forgetting not to rush.

Calm Is Cool

Calm is cool
And see, girl
I've learned yelling and screaming
Cussing and fussing
Only makes you look like a fool
So stand tall
Head high
Laugh that shit off
And tell them ppl bye
See you later
Adios
Cuz You Are the table
You Are the G.O.A.T
And we all know you're known for doing the
most

So take a step back
Breath in
Breath out
Queens inspire each other
Not throw blows for clout
And that man just needs love
Not a warden doing head counts
So remember
Calm is cool
Use your words like soul food
Let love be your biggest tool
Even in a world that's so cruel.

Can't Stop, Won't Stop

Can't stop, Won't stop
No matter how bad they plot
I Can't stop
No matter how bad I want to give up I continue
to rise to the top
And this time on my soul
I won't stop, I can't stop
Not until this shit drop
Not until I've collected every crop
Harvested every seed I've sown
And fed every bird I know.

Shawn "Gemini" Hayes

It'll always be the 5th for me
That day you broke my heart
That day I woke up to that call
Saying you were gone
That call that said they took your life
And left you in that hall
Top 5
All-star
They all come to mind
But nothing hits worse
Than seeing a creature so kind
Leave that church in a hearse
I wish I was there
Wish I never left
But the best feeling
Is knowing
I'll always have the best angel
Watching over me till death.

Free The Real

I lay here unable to truly feel your pain
How it feels to sit behind that cell
I can only fathom the frustrations that may
bring
Lights Out
Head Count
And the continuous lack of privacy
Those fucked up conditions
With literally a pot to piss in
No fucking air condition
Like where does the money really go for these
prisons
Guards who treat you like shit
And expect you to respect 'em

Jealous inmates you can't trust around a weapon
Never really feeling fully protected
I hate that for you
That's why I scream "Free you!" till my face
turns blue.

Sit With It

Again and again, I sit with the discomfort.
Allowing it to be. Feeling it. Observing it.
Noticing the sensations in my body:
The heavy feeling in my chest.
The pit in my stomach. My skin feels like it's
crawling. A feeling of screaming within. I notice
my breathing change. I notice my temperature
change. I notice the thoughts that are triggered
by this discomfort. Bringing up old thought
patterns once more. I notice my mind trying to
wrestle with it.
Trying to make sense of why and how to stop it.

But I remind myself to remain still and just observe.

Taking deep breaths. Allowing it to be. Not running from it or trying to numb it. Because when discomfort is met with resistance, it creates a much greater war within.

And each time I sit with the discomfort, it feels like my capacity to handle it grows. I'm able to start seeing myself outside of the discomfort. Resting deeper into the awareness. To even be able to say, "I feel so uncomfortable," is to acknowledge that there is an "I" beyond the discomfort. That is aware of the discomfort. I myself am not discomfort. That "seeing" alone brings some freedom. It creates just a bit of space to see myself outside of my feelings and thoughts, which is all that discomfort is. Also, I feel like these thoughts and feelings are coming to the surface to be let go of.

Some may even call it grace.

It's okay, Just step outside

Whenever I feel alone
I just step outside
Where the wind wraps me in her loving arms
The sun gives me warm, gentle forehead kisses
Where trees wave hi
And the clouds tell me stories
As they pass me by
Where the birds serenade me
With beautiful melodies
And with permission to caress him
The grass grounds me like heaven's rays
So if you ever get lonely like I do at times
Just step outside and let Mother Nature love you
unconditionally from the inside.

Thank you tho

Girl, Don't text him
Let him call you first
Mannnn, Don't give her no money
She only a quick fuck
Show you care
But not too much
Fuck 'em good
But remember it's just a nut
Take her out to eat
But don't spend more than $40 bucks
On my soul this generation sucks
What happened to courting
What happened to chivalry
What happened to love

And why is it cool to pretend that a mf not weak
in the knees
Why is it okay to act like we wasn't just married
in these sheets
Like we wasn't just vibing to the beat
Man, I just want that old-school shit
That '90s r&b
Love you don't have to hide
Where nobody pretends
Or gets bad advice from their wack-ass friends
A slow love that heals and grows
So please don't tell me when to call
Or how to treat him
But thank you tho.

People Love Me

Yeah people love me
But only to a certain extent
Only 'til their demons start to twitch
Only until the words I speak start to sound
foreign
See, yeah, people love me
How could they not?
I'm the dope that feeds their mind until they
overdose off just one drop
The hope they see they can't just go out and cop
Oh wait I can also see why they sometimes hate
that they can't stop

I'm the fire that burns deep into their soul
The light revealing every insecurity, fear, and
flaw
They hide behind their masks, and hearts full of
stone
Yeah people love me
Question is, why am I always stuck wondering
for how long?
While feeling so alone….

Demons

Yeah demons came at me
And I greeted them with love and peace
They did their best to control me
But wasn't expecting to feel like they were
dying when they could no longer hold me
The main mission was to confuse and conquer
Not knowing I was sent to do the same
Hope you didn't think I was this pretty for the
fame
No, I was created this drop-dead gorgeous
So you would stop, look, and listen
To what he has to say—TMH that is

So yes the demons came
But I shined my light so bright
Loved them so right
And hugged them so tight
While praying over their souls through the night
They couldn't help but switch lanes
Throw in the towel and bow down to the King
In me that is
So when the demons ever come through
Remember they need love too
And really only want to play with the demons
inside you.

I Pray Everyone Finds Peace

I pray everyone finds peace
Lord I pray everybody finds happiness
I pray everyone heals
I pray everyone starts being their authentic self
and remove their veils
I pray all shame, hate, and the need to finesse
dies
And no not in vain
I pray that hurt brings gold into everyone's lives
I pray the earth transmutes all the pain into Love
I pray we all prevail
That way our kids can really live
And finally reach the stars above.

Scared

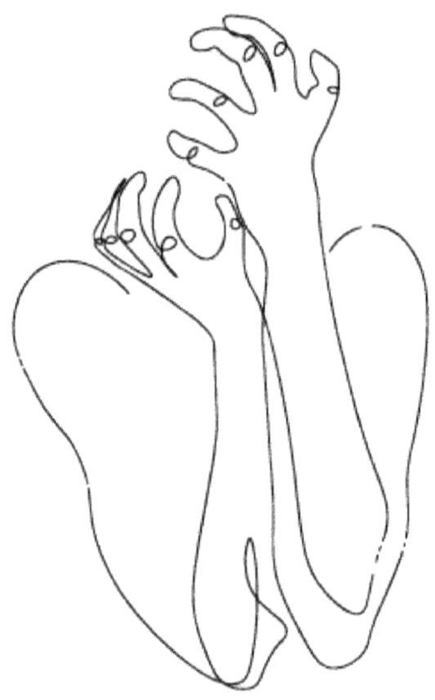

Scared to say what's on my mind
Because I'm terrified my words will be used
against me as trickery
Scared to just be me because everybody took
that as weak
Gullible, and Goofy
Instead of genuinely sweet
They chose to perceive me as a threat
Not just men but my own fucking family
My own fucking friends

The ones I thought I would have rode with 'til
the end
All played me
Took my kindness for weakness
All while plotting my downfall
The whole time I never would have thought—
Never saw the envy
Like they never saw the true friend in me
Or maybe they did
Maybe they cared
Or maybe that shit made them think I'd always
be there
Just to sit and fake it, just to say I had a friend
A mother or man……

Demons Pt2

Demons will protect you just as well as angels. If you only embrace them, instead of trying to cast them out. And before all the Christians start yelling and screaming at me in the name of Jesus! Please let me explain. Yes, some demons and spirits should be casted out expeditiously! But some demons are a part of you. A part of your destiny. A part of your soul mission. Sent to protect you in your lower states of consciousness. In the times when you just have to walk on the wild side. Either it be to have a good time doing ratchet things with your ratchet

friends, or doing what you need to survive. The demons are there to deceive and defend.
It's all about the choices you decide to make.
Can't keep blaming the devil…..

Real and Genuine

I couldn't stop texting
Cuz I told myself you were reading every word
I told myself you would make me a mixtape
from all the songs sent
I couldn't help recording myself
Cuz I needed you to see me
I needed you to feel every facial expression
Then maybe you would get it
Then maybe you would truly comprehend
Everything I was saying was real and genuine

......

3 days, 3 weeks

3 weeks and 3 days
And you're still the only one I want
Still the only one who has my main focus
Still the last one to steal my heart
And even tho I wish I could stop thinking bout u
Shit just keeps getting more insane
More intense
Making me less equipped to deal
With all these feelings and shit
At first I thought it was
Just cuz I hate hearing "no," Just cuz I wanted to
win
Just my desire
To be needed and wanted
Just cuz I hate starting all over again

But it's truly none of that at all
Honestly Idk what it is
Shit you don't even be giving me head
Don't buy me flowers
Ask me if I ate
Or take me out on dates
Guess it's cuz instead
You make me laugh
And ask me what I've read
How my day was
And actually care about what's going on in my
head
You Make time for me
When you really need it for yourself
And always run (well walk slowly)
When I need you most
Not to mention
The look in your eyes when we're laid up
And I'm the one eating breakfast in bed
So yes neither one of us may be perfect
Or ready
Or fully healed
But I honestly feel like you're perfect for me
So I'll be here stuck on you, I guess
Until one of us wakes up and sees.....

This Hurt

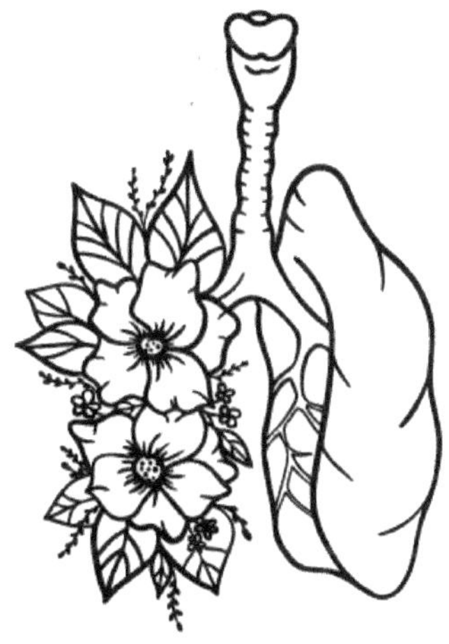

This hurt ain't really come from him
Naw this hurt really came from them
Yeah all them hoes I called my friends
All the bitches I called sis
All the fake smiles and hugs
I couldn't resist.....

July 31st

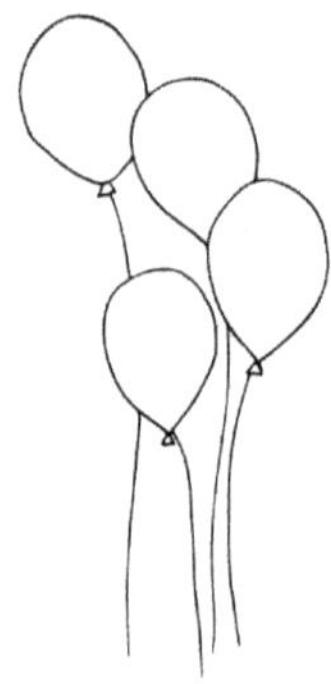

July 31st used to mean a lot to me
Now it just brings me pain and grief
And not because anybody died physically
But I had to kill 2 ppl mentally
Both my sisters—
One truly my blood
Emotionally betrayed by both
And today is also the day they both were born
2 different families
2 different versions
Of the same envious spirit
Just in a different vessels
Love them both to the death of me
Which persuaded me
To let them get the best of me
Trusted them with my deepest secrets

Whole time they were both secretly laughing
and exposing them
The list can go on
But I'm not here to bash
Just writing to let this shit go
Cuz see, I loved them bitches
Would have did 100 years for them bitches
But learned the hard way
They were never my bitches
Let alone my sisters
Or maybe they were
Guess we'll never know
Cuz like I said at the beginning of this poem
In my mind
Them bitches dead and gone
And water may not be thicker than blood
But know when shit gets deep
They both run…..

Devils on my back

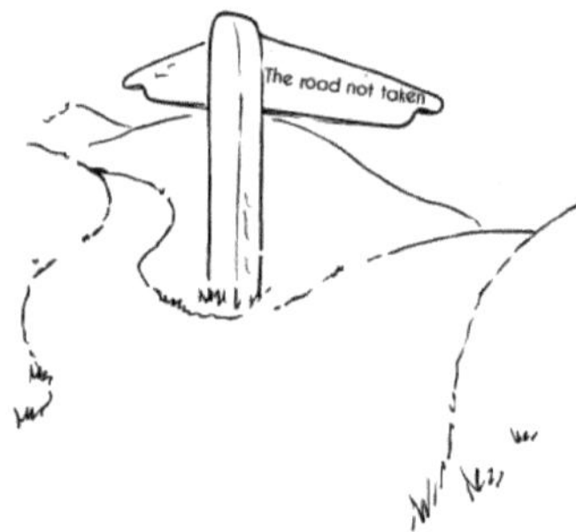

Devils on my back, Angels to my left
Chip on my shoulder
Love in my heart
Head held high
Standing Ten toes down
While I walk this lonely road
With a soul full of Gold
And faith as big as a mustard seed
Growing beautifully
Like a rose
Out of concrete
A cactus in the desert
Or a lotus straight out the mud

Envy

The lady who raised me envied me
That is why the words you say could never faze me
I was called all types of bitches
Constantly reminded of my flaws While being told I'd be nothing more Than a spitting image of my mother—"A crackhead whore"
So yes sticks and stones may break my bones
But see, your words are just words to me
Especially when I've been bullied by most of my family
Name dragged through the mud
And slandered by the ones closest to me
The ones chosen to be my protector And comfort me

Chosen to Lighten the load of this mystical
journey
Instead of training me to people please
And speak to myself negatively
So when you see my light and decide to hate/
envy me
Please remember
you're not the first
you won't be the last
And most importantly I always get the last laugh

I Love my own energy

I love my own energy
And that's why I'm content with being alone
1+1=2
And baby, I want but don't need you
I've learned how to love me enough for me and
you
So when you come it's to complement and add
Not piss me off and make me mad
But instead see the value hidden deep within my
head and not just inside my bed ….

I Walk

My ancestors used to sneak around
To walk these grounds
Now I walk 'em like a Boss
Yeah like when Jesus Christ carried his cross
With my head held high
I walk them loud I walk them Proud
I walk them without a care in the world for miles
and miles
So shoutout to my ancestors
Y'all the ones who deserve all the clout
Cuz without y'all, going against the grain
You know
Enduring all that pain

We would have never learned their dirty little
game
Never learned all the shit they was teaching us
Was super lame and just for fame
Our real legacy
Just all twisted and turned
Written in reverse
But see y'all knew our destiny was still on
course
And worth more than some gold in your mama's
purse
And yeah it took us a few decades
But we're finally figuring it out
So thank you for enduring all that pain
While still smiling through the rain
But most of all
Thank you for still crushing niggas from the
grave….. Ase

Broken soul

Saw your pure heart
And fell in love with your broken soul
The glow in your eyes
Shined brighter than gold
Yet I could still feel the Ice-cold blood
Running through your veins
From all the hurt
All the betrayal
All the regret
All the pain
Every tear you've dropped,
 Every fight you've fought,
I could feel it all
While you wore your mask

Acting like it was what it was not
So I walked away
Because I refused to be the one
Who paid for the way
They plotted and played you
While trying to trick you out of your spot I
refuse
And I will not
What I will do is love you till I drop
Love you like no one has ever loved you before
Love you like I wished they would have loved
me more
Cuz see my blood is ice-cold too
I just learned how to grow and love through and
through.

Alone Again

Alone again
Laying here all in my dome again
Looking down at this phone again
Thought this one was him
Guess I was wrong again
God please tell me why you said no again?
Like why he had to go like them?
Why tf I gotta sit here and be strong again?
God I'm just so ready to love again
Hug again, Laugh again
And God not just when we begin
But over and over and over again
Until our souls leave and return again

Man o man

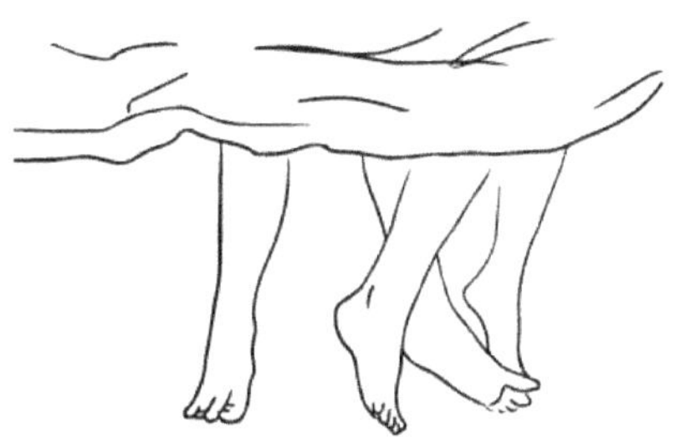

Man o man
How I miss that ass
Man I miss you bad
I miss you your laugh
I miss your smile
I miss your touch
Man honestly
I just miss the way we used to converse
Man o Man
I fucking miss you
Your accent
Your style
Even your stubborness
I miss it I miss it
I miss it all
Especially the way you used to stand tall

Late at night when you had me pinned against
the wall
Man o man
How I miss licking your balls
I fucking miss it all…..

Rather you say No

I'd rather you say no
Then pop up when you need me close
Rather you hurt my feelings
Than lead me on
Rather be your best friend first
That way we don't come to a crashing end
I'd rather you tell me the ugly truth
Over any pretty lie
I'd rather you be free
More than I'd rather be in love
I'd rather we both live
Before we'd ever rather want to die…..

Pick a Side

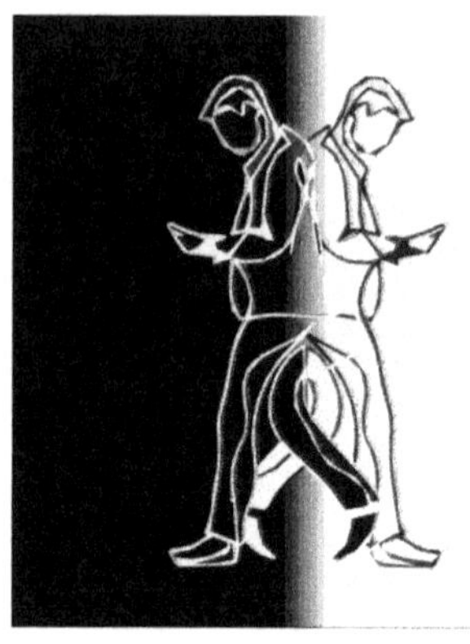

Too hard to pick a side
Especially when I don't even know
How I became tossed between y'all's pride
Therefore
I choose mine
Which in the end leads me to sleep outside
Outside my comfort zone
Outside my need to be loved
Naw fr tho I'm writing this at 5:55 While the
doves sing
And the sun begins to rise
High Above my city's demise
Searching for a safe place to hide
Somewhere besides
Hiding behind enemy lines
Somewhere no one can hear my cries

While I reflect on all the beautiful lies
Out the way of all them soul ties
Some place where Gods thrive
And the devil dies……

Worth The Wait

Fucking with you comes with a price.
Question is….
Am I willing to pay that price twice?
Honestly….
It depends on the measures.
Would I be willing to pay the price of my life?
No
Having a baby?
Maybe
Losing out on my soul mate?
Well see about that…..
What's for me is for me!
So yes I may delay my destiny
But losing my soul mate all together
That's just a bit extreme
Especially when I think your
"Really Him"
See what I did there

No but back to the question at hand
How far will I go, or do I continue to stand
Ten toes down on the business I planned
Or am I willing to lose more sleep
More tears or more weight from the lack of
wanting to eat
Or crying until my eyes look weak
Right now in this moment I feel like that's small
shit to reap
And honestly I was doing all that cuz I was a
small bitch to me
I let your presence or lack thereof define who I
was
When my presence is the gift of love
Damn now I forget what the question was….

My Ancestors

I read because it was once illegal for MY
ANCESTORS to do so
I speak up because THEY once told MY
ANCESTORS to be silent
I stand tall because THEY used to beat MY
ANCESTORS down to their knees
I stand on business because MY ANCESTORS
marched day and night
Just for my generation to even be able to achieve
great things and fight
I sit where I want on the bus but especially at the
front
To pay my homage—
For Rosa Parks was no punk
I walk for miles sometimes just to internalize the
pride hidden behind their smiles

I love how my ancestors loved despite the hate
and distrust
So I will forever do the same
For it runs deep in my blood

What A Shame

What a shame
I hurt your pride and ego
So now things will never be the same
You'll never look at me like an angel ever again
You'll just see the woman who made you feel
shame
The only woman who saw past your pain
The bitch who made you regret your selfish
ways
The bitch who refused to play your childish little
games
The one who just wanted to help you heal
The one who just wanted to take all of our
broken pieces and build

Yeah such a shame
You chose me to blame
When I was just trying to stay in my lane
Instead you chose to paint me out to be the lame
All because you were to scared to gain
A woman who loved the man behind the mask
A woman way more than just a plain Jane

While You Sleep

I pray over you while you sleep
So it's okay to run
Cuz I know them demons you fight
Whooping your ass bout me
Putting that wool over your eyes
So you can't see
The divine connection we could have
If you just let be
The love and prosperity
It could all be so simple
Or whatever Lauren hill said
But you run forest, run

Run until you know your done
Run until you know without a doubt
You feel the chemistry
You feel the sparks
You want the loyalty
You want my heart
Until you know for sure you never want to part
Cuz I'm tired of praying for the best
Just to end up feeling like less….

9 789363 309913